The Stars Went Out and So Did the Moon

poems by

Cristiana Baik

Finishing Line Press
Georgetown, Kentucky

The Stars Went Out and So Did the Moon

Copyright © 2017 by Cristiana Baik
ISBN 978-1-63534-329-8 First Edition
All rights reserved under International and Pan-American Copyright Conventions.
No part of this book may be reproduced in any manner whatsoever without written permission from the publisher, except in the case of brief quotations embodied in critical articles and reviews.

ACKNOWLEDGMENTS

"Birthday" appears in *TYPO* (October 2016)
"Winter Solstice" appears in *Witness* (Winter 2016)
"10/1" appears in *Dusie* (Winter 2016)
"Falsework" appeared in the *Spinning Jenny* (Issue 10, 2007)
"Lethe" appeared in *American Letters & Commentary* (Issue 20, 2008)
"Semi-Fluorescence" appeared in *Conjunctions* (2008)
"Objet Trouvé" and "Autoconstrucción" appeared in *Apogee Journal* (2015)

Publisher: Leah Maines

Editor: Christen Kincaid

Cover Art: Somya Singh

Author Photo: Crystal Baik

Cover Design: Elizabeth Maines McCleavy

Printed in the USA on acid-free paper.
Order online: www.finishinglinepress.com
       also available on amazon.com

               Author inquiries and mail orders:
                      Finishing Line Press
                        P. O. Box 1626
                Georgetown, Kentucky 40324
                          U. S. A.

Table of Contents

Birthday 1

Adultery 2

Lethe 4

Falsework 5

Map (i) 6

10/1 7

Surgical Heart (I) 8

Apology 9

Yield 10

Surgical Heart (II) 11

Map (ii) 12

Intimacy 13

Semi-Fluorescence 15

Winter Solstice 17

Semblance 18

After Icarus 19

Calcareous 20

Some Weather Coming 21

Seek 22

Objet Trouvé 23

*For my beloveds: Crystal, Coleen, Lily, Jillian, Sarah D
To uhm-mah and uppah: thank you for
all the unspoken sacrifices*

Birthday

Blame it on the mercurial crossing.
As a child, my parents moved home the distance of the ocean.
As a child, sleeping away loss, the plane over the Pacific
in the dark, making its way toward the solar eclipse
like a dedicated lover.
It all feels like a late yesterday.
Now towarding the border of a creek
the sun's light retracting on the loveliness
of a new face, the mist ghosting the Pacific.
Something is always fleeting.
Is it fearing what I'm likely to miss—
you who have always been a stranger.
The memories that move in your ghost tonight.
Feeling dizzy and dazed, the way my head feels
after too many glasses of champagne,
toasting to a long lost birthday.
Nothing fits
so barehanded I will love
what is splintered, this lantern of our
post-flammable home.

Adultery

(i) *Say the time of moon is not right for escape*
Here I sleep in a stranger's bed.
You don't mind. You
keep rearranging bedroom furniture—a nightstand
transforms into a window, 4 pm light
flight, gleaming, to barrage corners of the bedroom
walls, all shoring up to splinter. Golden rim,
a clumsy core terrain. So
what sort of illusion is this, a body
always shimmering
to splinter.

(ii) *Three trees were maimed on their account, and I am keeping count*

It is in this dream that you murder her birds.
Flock's headlong flight into the forestry's tapestry,
       saw-toothed, landing shadows—
resembling light-breach, tethered
in storm, aloft
like sere branches,
like a Jacob's
ladder.

(iii)   *How fast can you live?*

    In my dream, he takes the last question.
    This room remnant
    I stand in is a dark hall.
    I can't see him, but his voice is there,
    echoing to eat air, a thrust-gesture
    so mashing that I get
    dizzy just writing about it. I look
    for him
    past the backyard
    horizon, past the snared, snarled wood
    arriving light latticing the fence.
    The neighbor's dog sleeps
    cold in shadows beneath the late drawn
    sun. This evening towards the peeling,
    wiped sky—a scarred, hazed-over
    thing. The wind-whaps
    burglar my arms, hands, face.
    This present is how it has always been.
    This, I realize, is the point
    of the dream.

Lethe

Up close, a body of water alters
into indivisible distance.
In parting, we don't feel exact speeds
or temperatures
but duration, our laxed bodies
submerging. When
entitlement over the other subsides
we swim with the movement
of a sharper blade, the tiny violence
mysterious but absolute. Before
a world of water—leaving—
we keep everything in sight.

~

Light will soften the response.
Like water, change alters indiscriminately.

~

Imagine the last question we might have asked:
 What were the factors that lead us to this?

Falsework

come to think who you are wild remnant lacking salt particles
split and there is no accolade to rupture. let me try it this way
you say. let me try to knapsack the weight
the rope unleashing, the ground noiseless. the sky to scoop you
the sky to rack you, the way to sleep you, to demand you, to crave you,
to diminish to haunt you. sleeping like a den and puncture. skirmish
and spar the lengths that make us. the lengths that sleep in concave,
not knowing when to diminish not knowing how to be just make.
making and punish, to alleviate nothing. slum to slavish the impulse,
desire, wanting to fling it back to construct an indestructible wall.

Map (i)

black threads
      hanging
glove-moon
lemon tree, leaves folded
      like torn paper into brown earth,
a carpet of rot.
        list the domestic details   (trying to escape—
            a butter knife crashed into the sink
        good china consumed by dust
     light peeling away the living room
          the undisturbed painting of the lucky green heron
              about to take flight.
in bruised light she sits, her singular figure—
           mother waiting in the living room
for him. the eldest waits at the top of the stairs
     as the young ones sleep. they are told to stay in bed by the eldest.
father walks
in)
          her fist
           a warm, fragile shell, like leaf litter frayed in the sun.
his fist—an un/godly weight of stone,
     a freight disruption—thick plate. breaking
glass in our home a ritual like breaking bread.
       shouting a hard-lipped prayer
          towards the window
          to shut off the sky.

10/1

Cold flash of stars: altering wind, the direction wagoning: tulip trees, liriodendron tulipifera: still water of the harbor, a quiet place for me: today, desire compacted into trademarks: Just do it (™): Think Different (™): Don't Leave Home Without It (™): yet its *hiraeth* (n.), it has always been *hiraeth*: language an untranslatable context: subterranean wound: each breath rhizomic, regenerating our lace-mesh bodies, ever diaphanous, ever wind-broken: say memory or the act of remembering is the attempt to re-story the better self: take a moment to note the way light moves on the mattress, in the morning, next to one another, you pointing to the beads of rain devouring the window pane: a poem as a long stretch of thinking: bone, teeth, wound of the thing: celebrating, edging the universal sea: as branches loosen like lost pages; looking up at the singular leaves.

Surgical Heart (I)

Kin of hearts.
This is how you practice separation.

In full knowledge,
a recognition: restoration: rehabilitation: realization.

Giving thanks to this twin trumpet
of sorrow/relief.

My heart's landscape is a vast open country.

All the while shadows loosen and fall.
Fireflies buzz; tulips open

in the dark.
All the while

my left foot has fallen
asleep.

Is this what it's like?
Reaching home.

Tonight, through the trees
the submitting lights

of stars cry a ring.
I look and look

the sky wide-eyed, wind-wept,
and aloft.

Apology

there are opportunities: shutter
left open   moon-snared
haunted by uncertainty: that rim chance
              longing
shedding still into the record
of a lone crescent.
when he apologizes
your skin crawls.
you cough.
you must run for cover,
the wool in your mouth
to keep you from saying—your teeth
clenched, needle-halt before a firing squad.
in this dream of a bright white gap,
and in another dream, climbing through the sweat
and faint pink glare of monsoon heat.
you come to the slow-gun conclusion
in anticipation of the ghost, hidden yet not vanquished:
his dumb, dry voice
that jostles and draws
tightly—and when you wake the breath of the other
who you recall—
as your lover now breathes
shells of dissolve into your ear.

Yield

to know
when I look out
to describe this Friday
morning as calcified
I mean it hard
bare at the throat
a deposit of rusty dreams
where I run
led first by my collarbone
a corroded language
folding like a fist in my throat
understanding the concept
but not the mechanics of prayer
understanding the concept
but not the mechanics of devotion
so I will begin simply
with the view
of this, a bare maple tree
and a mourning dove.

Surgical Heart (II)

Camouflaged. Caught. Compressed. Spilled, spilling. Bent. Frangibled. Shed. Dispossessed. Hammered. Warned. Stumbling. Defiant. Poltergeisted. Enclaved. Succreased. Silhouetted. Energized. Struck. Splayed. Circumstanced. Continued, continuing. Pallored. Opened. Returned, returning. Fevered. Enormous-ified. Aleatoric-fied. Mandible-fied. Sprawled. Inwarded. Unfastened. Flame-framed. Untied. Split. Planted. Windowed. Quarried. Turned. Branched. Hued. Saturated. Extended. Cleaned. Lit. Lit.

Map (ii)

mother sleeps
                    the eldest sweeps
glass shards
     she buries
underneath the lemon tree.
              dug up, years later, they have transformed
             into smooth arrowheads
        reflecting the morning light
            a hazy yellow gauzing glass
      and resembling a crooked arm, a crescent moon
      refracting the afternoon's
      sunlit pond.

Intimacy

We text about Brexit
how a friend and her family will manage

change, how
referendum means loss

of a union, refortifying
imaginary borders because

they had no other plan
for what could come

next. You then describe
how our bodies worked

that afternoon—inrush
of hotel room light, mid-day,

you leaning whole
against me, my shoulders

mapping the wall,
warm air currenting

between our bodies.
After, my hands idly

brush curtains
casting shadows, sunlight tracking

the day
towards the hour
I leave.

In the plane
I dream

my body's shape a tear
with summer water

rushing bulrushes
and dry grass

water gathering
long inlets

to become a singular swell
softening

so it is impossible
to describe where our borders

begin or end.

Semi-Fluorescence

Good night air glows

under the quantum

quiet fury

of these southern

stars. You

drive

restless

on the interstate

hoping not to lose

yourself. The stars have you

tonight

setting aglow

a back road in Kentucky. Unnamed

so you name it

Nantucket, as you

doubly

mismatch real life images—
the long grass and rifles, displaced

by occasional rain,

duties and responses sidelined

by laundry lines, the loose

black nylon

drifting.

Winter Solstice

in winterkilled
grass you find an arrowhead
your knees locked in dirt
saying *look what I found.*
tonight the planet leans toward its star.
if I listen better
I'll hear you, each time
your head turns, expectations,
moonlight washing
sidewalk, lawns, roofs
on this the briefest day/longest night
of the year. straightening elbows
you smooth away the dirt
holding the arrowhead to the palm
like a consequence
a great secret half-forgotten.
we start home moving slowly
and in sleep return to a dream assembly
of questions, always an unfinished calling
and an open window.

Semblance

it was a day-long
tender—microwave-blue
clouds, fall
light tipping
leaves, me
breaking in birthday's new
winter boots. after you
left, I noticed
the first frost netting
aspens, as I lingered
late in the last
of fall's chandelier
light.

After Icarus

darkening dusk,
moon's phantom slinks
to eat the age of rust
from swings swung by bristling
wind fracturing shadows
onto rolling leaves. we smoke
in dampened grass
each blade's singular
length of silence
impressing into our worked
and worn palms. the horizon recedes, as blue-tarred,
half-stars advance. in the dark, we marvel
at moths' iridescent
desire for contact
towards that singular source (*are humans
really that different*), their tin-sheen wings flashing
bursts in stadium light.

Calcareous

here in the desert
night crawls towards
its hour with radial-ice
threading windows.
snow's last drifts knuckle
dolostones, these wind-wrecked
corruptions, imperfect and overwhelming.
so many miles driven, so much sky, the climb
up the range, entangled by wind. the sense
that this was *real* air, a skin
of the present. taproots of trees,
their splintering
bark eaten by the ages but still
standing in rare air.
she thought about what her eyes
could no longer remember,
half-remembered faces
like delicate tracings
undersiding leaves.
This faded map
of a place I
have explored all my life.

Some Weather Coming

to fish, spiders, & sweater: fall's first full day has arrived.
to sleep, paper, & shelter: I write into the morning's margins,
sun pale at my back.
wind-crawls, stalking everywhere.
fin-flurries of fish: October's restlessness.
same questions, different questions surface, scatter, & flee.
as on the skin of water, petals, leaves, & feathers ghost-multiply.

Seek

flatten your body against
the trunk, stretching
into it, a reduction
into the lean. listen
for sounds of fledglings,
last bells splitting the air.
stand on leaf-cover's
parchment, all snaps of limbless
& leafless.
sun's a burnished fescue:
penny warm and rusted in the pocket,
slow sap signing onto
your fingertips. alone,
in this open-mouthed landscape,
mock-orange and echo,
you predict
it will have been a brief year
but a long winter:
home's flickering lights
and a door opening,
seeking luck
in the shadows
of a sleepless,
faceless full moon.

Objet Trouvé

Midafternoon hour's changing light,
fetching. Thunderstorms in distance
resemble washed-over paintings, blue
sanded down pale. In a dream, there
were no roads, not even paths. Just
piled-up stones, where trees
began to grow. In another dream a hat,
obsidian, wire mesh. Broken shells
and plastic buoys. Hula-hoops. He said
This is an encounter, all the while I thought
it impasse, watching the delicate rupture, flood
of light gradually darkening into vast open
space. Then I was left with found fragments,
possibilities after points of convergence,
an invisible force becoming equilibrium. I told him
there was never enough discipline
only shared language.

Cristiana Baik was born in Seoul, South Korea, and raised by the coast in Southern California. She received her MFA from the University of Alabama-Tuscaloosa, and her BA in Cultural Anthropology and Gender Studies from the University of Chicago.

Her poems and book reviews have been published online and in various literary journals, including *The Conversant, Essay Press (forthcoming), TYPO, Dusie, Apogee Journal, Conjunctions*, among other publications. Currently, she works as the Director of Development at San Francisco's Richmond Area Multi-Services, Inc.

www.ingramcontent.com/pod-product-compliance
Lightning Source LLC
LaVergne TN
LVHW041520070426
835507LV00012B/1714